ESSENTIAL
Italian

p

Contents

Introduction

The thought of Italian cooking conjures up images of flavoursome olive oil, fresh vegetables and pasta, which is probably why Italian food is a favourite world-wide. Good-food lovers can enjoy the healthy aspect of this cuisine, which while being substantial boasts low cholesterol and saturated fat levels and is abound with vitamins.

The richness and variety of the country's cuisine can be identified by its regions, each having its own speciality. There are two main culinary zones in Italy: the wine and olive zone, which lies around Umbria, Liguria and the south; and the cattle country, where the olive tree will not flourish – Emilia-Romagna, Lombardy and Veneto – but where milk and butter are widely produced. However, more locally the food is influenced by the produce grown and caught. For example, the Veneto region is renowned for serving polenta with almost everything, while the national dish of Sardinia is the suckling pig.

There are some ingredients which are national favourites all over Italy and this should be kept in mind when cooking Italian. The rich plum tomato is always a favourite brightening any dish and adding a sweet flavour. Extra virgin olive oil is a necessity and it is worth investing in a high quality product as this is not only healthier but also adds a more authentic flavour. Herbs are particularly important in achieving an Italian-tasting dish, the principal ones being basil, oregano, rosemary, and thyme.

The ingredients are not the only reason why Italian food is so appealing. The country's gastronomy encourages outdoor living, lazy evenings, good wine and excellent company. The cuisine can be enjoyed by both the vegetarian and meat-lover alike and there are dishes for any time of day, whether it be a light midday snack or a sumptuous evening meal. *Essential Italian* contains recipes that will bring the Mediterranean flavour to your table whenever you desire, there are soups that can be eaten as starters and those which can be served as the main meal. There are hearty meat dishes for a winter's night and salads for a summer's evening.

Italian meals need not be expensive. For those days when a quick and easy dish is required pasta always satisfies. It is an excellent source of carbohydrate with endless possibilities for sauces and with over 200 varieties. Some of the most authentic dishes have been selected such as minestrone and spaghetti alla carbonara. Rice dishes are also very popular in the north of Italy, where risottos are extremely common. The best type of rice is Arborio, which should be rinsed before using. An Italian risotto is far moister than pilau and should not be served soggy.

Minestrone

Serves 8–10

INGREDIENTS

3 garlic cloves

3 large onions

2 celery sticks (stalks)

2 large carrots

2 large potatoes

100 g/3½ oz French (green)
  beans

100 g/3½ oz courgettes
  (zucchini)

60 g/2 oz/4 tbsp butter

50 ml/2 fl oz/¼ cup olive oil

60 g/2 oz rindless fatty bacon,
  finely diced

1.5 litres/2¾ pints/6⅞ cups
  vegetable or chicken stock

100 g/3½ oz chopped tomatoes

2 tbsp tomato purée (paste)

1 bunch fresh basil, finely
  chopped

100 g/3½ oz Parmesan
  cheese rind

85 g/3 oz dried spaghetti,
  broken up

salt and pepper

freshly grated Parmesan cheese,
  to serve

1 Finely chop the garlic, onions, celery, carrots, potatoes, beans and courgettes (zucchini).

2 Heat the butter and oil together in a large saucepan, add the bacon and cook for 2 minutes. Add the garlic and onion and fry for 2 minutes, then stir in the celery, carrots and potatoes and fry for a further 2 minutes.

3 Add the beans to the pan and fry for 2 minutes. Stir in the courgettes (zucchini) and fry for a further 2 minutes. Cover the pan and cook all the vegetables, stirring frequently, for 15 minutes.

4 Add the stock, tomatoes, tomato purée (paste), basil, and cheese rind and season to taste. Bring to the boil, lower the heat and simmer for 1 hour. Remove and discard the cheese rind.

5 Add the spaghetti pieces to the pan and cook for 20 minutes. Serve in large, warm soup bowls sprinkled with freshly grated Parmesan cheese.

Haricot (Navy) Bean & Pasta Soup

Serves 4

INGREDIENTS

250 g/9 oz/1⅓ cups haricot (navy) beans, soaked for 3 hours in cold water and drained

4 tbsp olive oil

2 large onions, sliced

3 garlic cloves, chopped

425 g/14 oz can chopped tomatoes

1 tsp dried oregano

1 tsp tomato purée (paste)

850 ml/1½ pints/3½ cups water

90 g/3½ oz/¾ cup dried fusilli or conchigliette

115 g/4 oz sun-dried tomatoes, drained and thinly sliced

1 tbsp chopped fresh coriander (cilantro) or flat leaf parsley

salt and pepper

2 tbsp Parmesan cheese shavings, to serve

1 Put the haricot (navy) beans in a large pan. Cover with cold water and bring to the boil. Boil vigorously for 15 minutes. Drain and keep warm.

2 Heat the oil in a pan over a medium heat and fry the onions for 2–3 minutes or until soft. Stir in the garlic and cook for 1 minute. Stir in the tomatoes, oregano and tomato purée (paste).

3 Add the water and the reserved beans to the pan. Bring to the boil, cover, then simmer for about 45 minutes, or until the beans are almost tender.

4 Add the pasta to the pan and season to taste. Stir in the sun-dried tomatoes, bring back to the boil, partly cover and simmer for 10 minutes, or until the pasta is tender, but still firm to the bite.

5 Stir the herbs into the soup. Ladle the soup into warm serving bowls, sprinkle with Parmesan and serve.

COOK'S TIP

If preferred, place the beans in a pan of cold water and bring to the boil. Remove from the heat and leave the beans to cook in the water. Drain and rinse before using.

Cream of Lemon & Chicken Soup with Spaghetti

Serves 4

INGREDIENTS

60 g/2 oz/4 tbsp butter
8 shallots, thinly sliced
2 carrots, thinly sliced
2 celery sticks (stalks), thinly sliced
225 g/8 oz boned chicken breasts, finely chopped
3 lemons

1.2 litres/2 pints/5 cups chicken stock
225 g/8 oz dried spaghetti, broken into small pieces
150 ml/^{1}/4 pint/^{5}/8 cup double (heavy) cream
salt and white pepper

TO GARNISH:
fresh parsley sprig
3 lemon slices, halved

1 Melt the butter in a large saucepan. Add the shallots, carrots, celery and chicken and cook over a low heat, stirring occasionally, for 8 minutes.

2 Thinly pare the lemons and blanch the lemon rind in boiling water for 3 minutes. Squeeze the juice from the lemons.

3 Add the lemon rind and juice to the pan, together with the chicken stock. Bring slowly to the boil over a low heat and simmer for 40 minutes.

4 Add the spaghetti to the pan and cook for 15 minutes. Season with salt and white pepper and add the cream. Heat through, but do not allow the soup to boil.

5 Pour the soup into a tureen or individual bowls, garnish with the parsley and half slices of lemon and serve immediately.

COOK'S TIP

You can prepare this soup up to the end of step 3 in advance, so that all you need do before serving is heat it through before adding the pasta and the finishing touches.

Mussel & Potato Soup

Serves 4

INGREDIENTS

750 g/1 lb 10 oz mussels
2 tbsp olive oil
100 g/3¹/₂ oz/7 tbsp unsalted
  butter
2 slices rindless, fatty bacon,
  chopped
1 onion, chopped
2 garlic cloves, crushed
60 g/2 oz/¹/₂ cup plain

(all purpose) flour
450 g/1 lb potatoes, thinly sliced
100 g/3¹/₂ oz/³/₄ cup
  dried conchigliette
300 ml/¹/₂ pint/1¹/₄ cups double
  (heavy) cream
1 tbsp lemon juice
2 egg yolks
salt and pepper

TO GARNISH:
2 tbsp finely chopped fresh
  parsley
lemon wedges

1 Debeard the mussels and scrub them under cold water for 5 minutes. Discard any mussels that do not close immediately when sharply tapped.

2 Bring a large pan of water to the boil, add the mussels, oil and a little pepper and cook until the mussels open.

3 Drain the mussels, reserving the cooking liquid. Discard any mussels that are closed. Remove the mussels from their shells.

4 Melt the butter in a large saucepan and cook the bacon, onion and garlic for 4 minutes. Stir in the flour, then 1.2 litres/2 pints/5 cups of the reserved cooking liquid.

5 Add the potatoes to the pan and simmer for 5 minutes. Add the conchigliette and simmer for a further 10 minutes.

6 Add the cream and lemon juice, season to taste, then add the mussels to the pan.

7 Blend the egg yolks with 1-2 tbsp of the remaining cooking liquid, stir into the pan and cook for 4 minutes.

8 Ladle the soup into 4 warm individual soup bowls, garnish with the chopped fresh parsley and lemon wedges and serve.

Spaghetti alla Carbonara

Serves 4

INGREDIENTS

425 g/15 oz dried spaghetti
2 tbsp olive oil
1 large onion, thinly sliced
2 garlic cloves, chopped
175 g/6 oz rindless bacon, cut
    into thin strips
25 g/1 oz/2 tbsp butter

175 g/6 oz mushrooms, thinly
    sliced
300 ml/½ pint/1¼ cups double
    (heavy) cream
3 eggs, beaten
100 g /3½ oz/1 cup freshly
    grated Parmesan cheese, plus

extra to serve (optional)
salt and pepper
fresh sage sprigs, to garnish

---

1 Warm a large serving dish or bowl. Bring a large pan of lightly salted water to the boil. Add the spaghetti and 1 tbsp of the oil and cook until tender, but still firm to the bite. Drain, return to the pan and keep warm.

2 Heat the remaining oil in a frying pan (skillet) over a medium heat. Add the onion and fry until it is transparent. Add the garlic and bacon and fry until the bacon is crisp. Transfer to the warm dish.

3 Melt the butter in the frying pan (skillet). Add the mushrooms and fry, stirring occasionally, for 3–4 minutes. Return the bacon mixture to the pan. Cover and keep warm.

4 Mix together the cream, eggs and cheese in a large bowl and then season to taste with salt and pepper.

5 Working very quickly, tip the spaghetti into the bacon and mushroom mixture and pour over the eggs. Toss the spaghetti quickly into the egg and cream mixture, using 2 forks. garnish and serve with extra grated Parmesan cheese, if using.

COOK'S TIP

The key to success with this recipe is not to overcook the egg. That is why it is important to keep all the ingredients hot enough just to cook the egg and to work rapidly to avoid scrambling it.

Spaghetti with Ricotta Cheese

Serves 4

INGREDIENTS

350 g/12 oz dried spaghetti
3 tbsp olive oil
40 g/$1^{1}/_2$ oz/3 tbsp butter
2 tbsp chopped fresh flat leaf
    parsley
125 g/$4^{1}/_2$ oz/1 cup freshly
    ground almonds

125 g/$4^{1}/_2$ oz/$^{1}/_2$ cup ricotta
    cheese
pinch of grated nutmeg
pinch of ground cinnamon
150 ml/$^{1}/_4$ pint/$^{5}/_8$ cup crème
    fraîche (unsweetened yogurt)
125 ml/4 fl oz hot chicken stock

1 tbsp pine nuts (kernels)
salt and pepper
fresh flat leaf parsley sprigs,
    to garnish

1 Bring a large pan of lightly salted water to the boil. Add the spaghetti and 1 tbsp of the oil and cook until tender, but still firm to the bite.

2 Drain the pasta, return to the pan and toss with the butter and chopped parsley. Set aside and keep warm.

3 To make the sauce, mix together the ground almonds, ricotta cheese, nutmeg, cinnamon and crème fraîche (unsweetened yogurt) over a low heat to form a thick paste. Stir in the remaining oil, then gradually stir in the hot chicken stock, until smooth. Season to taste.

4 Transfer the spaghetti to a warm serving dish, pour over the sauce and toss together well (see Cook's Tip, right). Sprinkle over the pine nuts (kernels), garnish with the flat leaf parsley sprigs and serve warm.

COOK'S TIP

Use two large forks to toss spaghetti or other long pasta, so that it is thoroughly coated with the sauce. Special spaghetti forks are available from some cookware departments and kitchen shops. Holding one fork in each hand, gently ease the prongs under the pasta on each side and lift them towards the centre. Continue until the pasta is completely coated.

Sicilian Spaghetti

Serves 4

INGREDIENTS

150 ml/¼ pint/⅝ cup olive oil, plus extra for brushing
2 aubergines (eggplants)
350 g/12 oz/3 cups minced (ground) beef
1 onion, chopped
2 garlic cloves, crushed
2 tbsp tomato purée (paste)

400 g/14 oz can chopped tomatoes
1 tsp Worcestershire sauce
1 tsp chopped fresh marjoram or oregano or ½ tsp dried marjoram or oregano
60 g/2 oz/½ cup stoned (pitted) black olives, sliced

1 green, red or yellow (bell) pepper, cored, seeded and chopped
175 g/6 oz dried spaghetti
115 g/4 oz/1 cup freshly grated Parmesan cheese
salt and pepper

1 Brush a 20 cm/8 inch loose-based round cake tin (pan) with oil, line the base with baking parchment and brush with oil.

2 Slice the aubergines (eggplants). Fry the aubergines (eggplant) in a little oil until browned on both sides. Drain on kitchen paper (towels).

3 Cook the beef, onion and garlic in a pan, stirring, until browned. Add the tomato purée (paste), tomatoes, Worcestershire sauce, herbs and salt and pepper. Simmer for 10 minutes. Add the olives and (bell) pepper and cook for a further 10 minutes.

4 Bring a pan of salted water to the boil. Add the spaghetti and 1 tbsp olive oil and cook until tender. Drain and turn the spaghetti into a bowl. Add the meat mixture and cheese and toss to mix.

5 Arrange aubergine (eggplant) slices over the base and sides of the tin (pan). Add the pasta, then cover with the rest of the aubergine (eggplant). Bake in a preheated oven at 200°C/400°F/ Gas 6 for 40 minutes. Leave to stand for 5 minutes, then invert on to a serving dish. Discard the baking parchment and serve.

Pasticcio

Serves 6

INGREDIENTS

250 g/8 oz/2 cups dried fusilli
1 tbsp olive oil, plus extra
  for brushing
4 tbsp double (heavy) cream
mixed salad, to serve

SAUCE:
2 tbsp olive oil
1 onion, thinly sliced
1 red (bell) pepper, cored, seeded
  and chopped

2 garlic cloves, chopped
600 g/1 lb 5 oz/5¼ cups minced
  (ground) beef
400 g/14 oz can chopped
  tomatoes
125 ml/4 fl oz/½ cup dry white
  wine
2 tbsp chopped fresh parsley
60 g/2 oz can anchovies, drained
  and chopped
salt and pepper

TOPPING:
300 ml/½ pint/1¼ cups natural
  yogurt
3 eggs
pinch of freshly grated nutmeg
40 g/1½ oz/½ cup freshly grated
  Parmesan cheese

1 To make the sauce, heat the oil in a frying pan (skillet) and fry the onion and red (bell) pepper for 3 minutes. Add the garlic and cook for 1 minute. Add the beef and cook until browned.

2 Add the tomatoes and wine and bring to the boil. Simmer for 20 minutes, until thickened.

Stir in the parsley, anchovies and seasoning.

3 Bring a pan of salted water to the boil. Add the pasta and oil and cook for 10 minutes, until almost tender. Drain and transfer to a bowl. Stir in the cream.

4 For the topping, beat together the yogurt, eggs and nutmeg.

5 Brush an ovenproof dish with oil. Spoon in half the pasta and cover with half the meat sauce. Repeat, then spread over the topping and sprinkle with cheese.

6 Bake in a preheated oven at 190°C/375°F/ Gas 5 for 25 minutes until golden. Serve with a mixed salad.

Chicken & Wild Mushroom Lasagne

Serves 4

INGREDIENTS

butter, for greasing
14 sheets pre-cooked lasagne
850 ml/1¹/₂ pints/3³/₄ cups
    Béchamel Sauce
75 g/3 oz/1 cup grated
    Parmesan cheese

CHICKEN & WILD MUSHROOM
    SAUCE:
2 tbsp olive oil
2 garlic cloves, crushed
1 large onion, finely chopped
225 g/8 oz wild mushrooms,
    sliced
300 g/10¹/₂ oz/2¹/₂ cups minced
    (ground) chicken
80 g/3 oz chicken livers,
    finely chopped

115 g/4 oz Parma ham
    (prosciutto), diced
150 ml/¹/₄ pint/⁵/₈ cup Marsala
285g/10 oz can chopped
    tomatoes
1 tbsp chopped fresh basil leaves
2 tbsp tomato purée (paste)
salt and pepper

1 To make the sauce, heat the olive oil in a large saucepan. Add the garlic, onion and mushrooms and cook for 6 minutes.

2 Add the minced (ground) chicken, chicken livers and Parma ham (prosciutto) and cook for 12 minutes, until the meat has browned.

3 Stir the Marsala, tomatoes, basil and tomato purée (paste) into the pan and cook for 4 minutes. Season, cover and simmer for 30 minutes. Stir and simmer for a further 15 minutes.

4 Arrange the lasagne over the base of a greased ovenproof dish, spoon over a layer of

chicken and wild mushroom sauce, then a layer of Béchamel Sauce. Place another layer of lasagne on top and repeat the process twice, finishing with a layer of Béchamel Sauce. Sprinkle over the grated cheese and bake in a preheated oven at 190°C/375°F/Gas 5 for 35 minutes until golden brown. Serve immediately.

Chicken with Green Olives & Pasta

Serves 4

INGREDIENTS

4 chicken breasts, part boned
3 tbsp olive oil
25 g/1 oz/2 tbsp butter
1 large onion, finely chopped
2 garlic cloves, crushed
2 red, yellow or green (bell)
peppers, cored, seeded and
cut into large pieces

250 g/9 oz button mushrooms,
sliced or quartered
175 g/6 oz tomatoes, skinned
and halved
150 ml/¹/₄ pint/⁵/₈ cup dry
white wine
175 g/6 oz/1 ¹/₂ cups stoned
(pitted) green olives

4–6 tbsp double (heavy) cream
400 g/14 oz dried pasta
salt and pepper
chopped parsley, to garnish

1 Fry the chicken breasts in 2 tbsp of the oil and the butter until golden brown. Remove the chicken from the pan.

2 Add the onion and garlic to the pan and fry until beginning to soften. Add the (bell) peppers and mushrooms and cook for 2–3 minutes. Add the tomatoes and seasoning. Transfer the vegetables to a casserole with the chicken.

3 Add the wine to the pan and bring to the boil. Pour the wine over the chicken. Cover and cook in a preheated oven at 180°C/350°F/Gas 4 for 50 minutes.

4 Mix the olives into the casserole. Pour in the cream, cover and return to the oven for 10–20 minutes.

5 Meanwhile, bring a large pan of lightly salted water to the boil. Add the pasta and the remaining oil and cook until tender, but still firm to the bite. Drain the pasta well and transfer to a serving dish.

6 Arrange the chicken on top of the pasta, spoon over the sauce, garnish with the parsley and serve immediately. Alternatively, place the pasta in a large serving bowl and serve separately.

Farfalle with a Medley of Seafood

Serves 4

INGREDIENTS

12 raw tiger prawns (shrimp)
12 raw shrimp
125 g/4¹/₂ oz freshwater prawns
   (shrimp)
450 g/1 lb fillet of sea bream
60 g/2 oz/4 tbsp butter
12 scallops, shelled
juice and finely grated rind of
   1 lemon

pinch of saffron powder or
   threads
1 litre/1³/₄ pints/4 cups vegetable
   stock
150 ml/¹/₄ pint/⁵/₈ cup rose petal
   vinegar
450 g/1 lb dried farfalle
1 tbsp olive oil
150 ml/¹/₄ pint/⁵/₈ cup white wine

1 tbsp pink peppercorns
115 g/4 oz baby carrots
150 ml/¹/₄ pint/⁵/₈ cup double
   (heavy) cream or fromage
   frais
salt and pepper
fresh parsley, to garnish

1 Peel and devein the prawns (shrimp) and shrimp. Thinly slice the sea bream. Melt the butter in a pan, add the sea bream, scallops, prawns (shrimp) and shrimp and cook for 1–2 minutes.

2 Season with black pepper. Add the lemon juice and rind. Carefully add the saffron to the cooking juices (not to the seafood).

3 Remove the seafood from the pan, set aside and keep warm.

4 Return the pan to the heat and add the vegetable stock. Bring to the boil and reduce by one third. Add the rose petal vinegar and cook for 4 minutes, until reduced.

5 Bring a pan of salted water to the boil. Add the farfalle and olive oil and

cook until tender, but still firm to the bite. Drain and transfer to a serving plate, topped with the seafood.

6 Add the wine, peppercorns, and carrots to the pan and reduce the sauce for 6 minutes. Add the cream or fromage frais and simmer for 2 minutes. Pour the sauce over the seafood and pasta, garnish and serve.

Fettuccine all'Alfredo

Serves 4

INGREDIENTS

25 g/1 oz/2 tbsp butter
200 ml/7 fl oz/⅞ cup double
 (heavy) cream
460 g/1 lb fresh fettuccine
1 tbsp olive oil

90 g/3 oz/1 cup freshly grated
 Parmesan cheese, plus extra
 to serve
pinch of freshly grated nutmeg
salt and pepper

fresh parsley sprigs, to garnish

1 Put the butter and 150 ml/¼ pint/⅝ cup of the cream in a large saucepan and bring the mixture to the boil over a medium heat. Reduce the heat and then simmer gently for about 1½ minutes, or until slightly thickened.

2 Meanwhile, bring a large pan of lightly salted water to the boil. Add the fettuccine and olive oil and cook for 2–3 minutes, until tender but still firm to the bite. Drain the fettuccine, then pour over the cream sauce.

3 Using 2 forks, toss the fettuccine in the sauce over a low heat until thoroughly coated.

4 Add the remaining cream, the Parmesan cheese and nutmeg to the fettuccine mixture and season to taste. Toss thoroughly to coat while gently heating through.

5 Transfer the fettucine mixture to a warm serving plate and garnish with the fresh parsley sprigs. Serve immediately, handing extra grated Parmesan cheese separately.

VARIATION

This classic Roman dish is often served with the addition of strips of ham and fresh peas. Add 225 g/ 8 oz/2 cups shelled cooked peas and 175 g/6 oz ham strips with the Parmesan cheese in step 4.

Patriotic Pasta

Serves 4

INGREDIENTS

460 g/1 lb/4 cups dried farfalle
4 tbsp olive oil

460 g/1 lb cherry tomatoes
90 g/3 oz rocket (arugula)

salt and pepper
Pecorino cheese, to garnish

1 Bring a large saucepan of lightly salted water to the boil. Add the farfalle and 1 tbsp of the olive oil and cook until tender, but still firm to the bite. Drain the farfalle thoroughly and return to the pan.

2 Cut the cherry tomatoes in half and trim the rocket (arugula).

3 Heat the remaining olive oil in a large saucepan. Add the tomatoes and cook for 1 minute. Add the farfalle and the rocket (arugula) and stir gently to mix. Heat through and season to taste with salt and black pepper.

4 Meanwhile, using a vegetable peeler, shave thin slices of Pecorino cheese.

5 Transfer the farfalle and vegetables to a warm serving dish. Garnish with the Pecorino cheese shavings and serve immediately.

COOK'S TIP

Pecorino cheese is a hard sheep's milk cheese which resembles Parmesan and is often used for grating over a variety of dishes. It has a sharp flavour and is only used in small quantities.

COOK'S TIP

Rocket (arugula) is a small plant with irregular-shaped leaves rather like those of turnip tops (greens). The flavour is distinctively peppery and slightly reminiscent of radish. It has always been popular in Italy, both in salads and for serving with pasta and has recently enjoyed a revival in Britain and the United States, where it has now become very fashionable.

Fusilli, Avocado, Tomato & Mozzarella Salad

Serves 4

INGREDIENTS

2 tbsp pine nuts (kernels)
175 g/6 oz/1½ cups dried fusilli
1 tbsp olive oil
6 tomatoes
225 g/8 oz mozzarella cheese
1 large avocado pear

2 tbsp lemon juice
3 tbsp chopped fresh basil
salt and pepper
fresh basil sprigs, to garnish

DRESSING:
6 tbsp extra virgin olive oil
2 tbsp white wine vinegar
1 tsp wholegrain mustard
pinch of sugar

1 Spread the pine nuts (kernels) out on a baking (cookie) sheet and toast under a preheated grill (broiler) for 1–2 minutes. Remove and set aside to cool.

2 Bring a large saucepan of lightly salted water to the boil. Add the fusilli and olive oil and cook until tender, but still firm to the bite. Drain the pasta and refresh in cold water. Drain again and set aside to cool.

3 Thinly slice the tomatoes and the mozzarella cheese.

4 Cut the avocado pear in half, remove the stone (pit) and skin. Cut into thin slices lengthways and sprinkle with lemon juice to prevent discoloration.

5 To make the dressing, beat together all the dressing ingredients and season to taste with salt and black pepper.

6 Arrange the tomatoes, mozzarella cheese and avocado pear alternately in overlapping slices on a large serving platter.

7 Toss the pasta with half of the dressing and the chopped basil and season to taste. Spoon the pasta into the centre of the platter and pour over the remaining dressing. Sprinkle over the pine nuts (kernels), garnish with fresh basil sprigs and serve.

Tuscan Onion Soup

Serves 4

INGREDIENTS

50 g/1¾ oz pancetta ham, diced	850 ml/1¾ pints/3¾ cups hot	75 g/2¾ oz Gruyère or Cheddar
1 tbsp olive oil	chicken or ham stock	salt and pepper
4 large white onions, sliced	4 slices ciabatta or other	
thinly in rings	Italian bread	
3 garlic cloves, chopped	50 g/1¾ oz/3 tbsp butter	

1 Dry fry the pancetta in a large saucepan for 3–4 minutes until it begins to brown. Remove the pancetta from the pan and set aside until required.

2 Add the oil to the pan and cook the onions and garlic over a high heat for 4 minutes. Reduce the heat, cover and cook for 15 minutes until lightly caramelized.

3 Add the stock to the saucepan and bring to the boil. Reduce the heat and leave the mixture to simmer, covered, for about 10 minutes.

4 Toast the slices of ciabatta on both sides, under a preheated grill (broiler), for 2–3 minutes or until golden. Spread the ciabatta with butter and top with the Gruyère or Cheddar cheese. Cut the bread into bite-size pieces.

5 Add the reserved pancetta to the soup and season to taste with salt and pepper. Pour into 4 soup bowls and top with the toasted bread.

COOK'S TIP

Pancetta is similar to bacon, but it is air- and salt-cured for about 6 months. Pancetta is available from most delicatessens and some large supermarkets. If you cannot obtain pancetta use unsmoked bacon instead.

Creamy Tomato Soup

Serves 4

INGREDIENTS

50 g/1¾ oz/3 tbsp butter
700 g/1 lb 9oz ripe tomatoes,
    preferably plum, roughly
    chopped

850 ml/1½ pints/3¾ hot
    vegetable stock
150 ml/ 5 fl oz/2/3 cup milk or
    single (light) cream

50 g/1¾ oz/¼ cup ground
    almonds
1 tsp sugar
2 tbsp shredded basil leaves
salt and pepper

1 Melt the butter in a large saucepan. Add the tomatoes and cook for 5 minutes until the skins start to wrinkle. Season to taste with salt and pepper.

2 Add the stock to the pan, bring to the boil, cover and simmer for 10 minutes.

3 Meanwhile, under a preheated grill (broiler), lightly toast the ground almonds until they are golden-brown. This will take only 1-2 minutes, so watch them closely.

4 Remove the soup from the heat and place in a food processor and blend the mixture to form a smooth consistency. Alternatively, mash the soup with a potato masher.

5 Pass the soup through a sieve to remove any tomato skin or pips.

6 Place the soup in the pan and return to the heat. Stir in the milk or cream, ground almonds and sugar. Warm the soup through and add the shredded basil just before serving.

7 Transfer the creamy tomato soup to warm soup bowls and serve hot.

VARIATION

Very fine breadcrumbs can be used instead of the ground almonds, if you prefer. Toast them in the same way as the almonds and add with the milk or cream in step 6.

Tomatoes Stuffed with Tuna Mayonnaise

Serves 4

INGREDIENTS

4 plum tomatoes	4 tbsp olive oil	TO GARNISH:
2 tbsp sun-dried tomato paste	1 x 115g/4 oz can tuna, drained	2 sun-dried tomatoes, cut into
2 egg yolks	2 tbsp capers, rinsed	strips
2 tsp lemon juice	salt and pepper	fresh basil leaves
finely grated rind of 1 lemon		

1 Halve the tomatoes and scoop out the seeds. Divide the sun-dried tomato paste among the tomato halves and spread around the inside of the skin.

2 Place on a baking tray (cookie sheet) and roast in a preheated oven at 200°C/400°F/Gas Mark 6 for 12–15 minutes. Leave to cool slightly.

3 Meanwhile, make the mayonnaise. In a food processor, blend the egg yolks and lemon juice with the lemon rind until smooth. Once mixed and with the motor still running slowly, add the olive oil. Stop the processor as soon as the mayonnaise has thickened. Alternatively, use a hand whisk, beating the mixture continuously until it thickens.

4 Add the tuna and capers to the mayonnaise and season.

5 Spoon the tuna mayonnaise mixture into the tomato shells and garnish with sun-dried tomato strips and basil leaves. Return to the oven for a few minutes or serve chilled.

COOK'S TIP

For a picnic, do not roast the tomatoes, just scoop out the seeds, drain, cut-side down on absorbent kitchen paper for 1 hour, and fill with the mayonnaise mixture. They are firmer to handle and easier to eat with the fingers this way. If you prefer, shop-bought mayonnaise may be used instead – just stir in the lemon rind.

Fresh Figs with Parma Ham (Prosciutto)

Serves 4

INGREDIENTS

40 g/1¹⁄₂ oz rocket (arugula)	4 tbsp olive oil	1 tbsp clear honey
4 fresh figs	1 tbsp fresh orange juice	1 small red chilli
4 slices Parma ham (prosciutto)		

1 Tear the rocket (arugula) into more manageable pieces and arrange on 4 serving plates.

2 Using a sharp knife, cut each of the figs into quarters and place them on top of the rocket (arugula) leaves.

3 Using a sharp knife, cut the Parma ham (prosciutto) into strips and scatter over the rocket (arugula) and figs.

4 Place the oil, orange juice and honey in a screw-top jar. Shake the jar until the mixture emulsifies and forms a thick dressing. Transfer to a bowl.

5 Using a sharp knife, dice the chilli, remembering not to touch your face before you have washed your hands (see Cook's Tip, right). Add the chopped chilli to the dressing and mix well.

6 Drizzle the dressing over the Parma ham (prosciutto), rocket (arugula) and figs, tossing to mix well. Serve at once.

COOK'S TIP

Chillies can burn the skin for several hours after chopping, so it is advisable to wear gloves when you are handling the very hot varieties.

COOK'S TIP

Parma, in the Emilia-Romagna region of Italy, is famous for its ham, prosciutto di Parma, *thought to be the best in the world.*

Spinach Salad

Serves 4

INGREDIENTS

100 g/3½ oz baby spinach, washed
75 g/2¾ oz radicchio leaves,
    shredded
50 g/1¾ oz mushrooms

100 g/3½ oz cooked chicken,
    preferably breast
50 g/1¾ oz Parma ham
    (prosciutto)

2 tbsp olive oil
finely grated rind of ½ orange
    and juice of 1 orange
1 tbsp natural yogurt

1 Wipe the mushrooms with a damp cloth to remove any excess dirt.

2 Gently mix together the spinach and radicchio in a large salad bowl.

3 Thinly slice the wiped mushrooms and add them to the bowl containing the spinach and radicchio.

4 Tear the cooked chicken breast and Parma ham (prosciutto) into strips and mix them into the salad.

5 To make the dressing, place the olive oil, orange rind, juice and yogurt into a screw-top jar. Shake the jar until the mixture is well combined. Season to taste with salt and pepper.

6 Drizzle the dressing over the spinach salad and toss to mix well. Serve immediately.

VARIATION

Spinach is delicious when served raw. Try raw spinach in a salad garnished with bacon or garlicky croutons. The young leaves have a wonderfully sharp flavour.

COOK'S TIP

Radiccio is a variety of chicory (endive) originating in Italy. It has a slightly bitter flavour.

Roasted Seafood

Serves 4

INGREDIENTS

600 g/1lb 5oz new potatoes
3 red onions, cut into wedges
2 courgettes (zucchini), sliced
    into chunks

8 garlic cloves, peeled
2 lemons, cut into wedges
4 sprigs rosemary
4 tbsp olive oil

350 g/12oz shell-on prawns
    (shrimp), preferably uncooked
2 small squid, chopped into rings
4 tomatoes, quartered

1 Scrub the potatoes to remove any excess dirt. Cut any large potatoes in half. Place the potatoes in a large roasting tin (pan), together with the onions, courgettes (zucchini), garlic, lemon and rosemary.

2 Pour over the oil and toss to coat all of the vegetables in the oil.

3 Cook in a preheated oven, at 200°C/400°F/Gas Mark 6, for about 40 minutes, turning occasionally, until the potatoes are tender.

4 Once the potatoes are tender, add the prawns (shrimp), squid and tomatoes, tossing to coat them in the oil, and roast for 10 minutes. All of the vegetables should be cooked through and slightly charred for full flavour.

5 Transfer to serving plates and serve hot.

COOK'S TIP

Squid and octopus are great favourites in Italy and all around the Mediterranean.

VARIATION

Most vegetables are suitable for roasting in the oven. Try adding 450 g/1 lb pumpkin, squash or aubergine (eggplant), if you prefer.

Genoese Seafood Risotto

Serves 4

INGREDIENTS

1.2 litres/2 pints/5 cups hot fish or chicken stock	2 garlic cloves, chopped	2 tbsp chopped oregano, plus extra for garnishing
350 g/12 oz arborio (risotto) rice, washed	250 g/9 oz mixed seafood, preferably raw, such as prawns (shrimp), squid, mussels, clams	50 g/1³/₄ oz pecorino or Parmesan cheese, grated
50 g/1³/₄ oz/3 tbsp butter	and (small) shrimps	

1 In a large saucepan, bring the stock to the boil. Add the rice and cook for about 12 minutes, stirring, until the rice is tender or according to the instructions on the packet. Drain thoroughly, reserving any excess liquid.

2 Heat the butter in a large frying pan (skillet) and add the garlic, stirring.

3 Add the raw mixed seafood to the pan (skillet) and cook for 5 minutes. If the seafood is already cooked, fry for 2–3 minutes.

4 Stir the oregano into the seafood mixture in the frying pan (skillet).

5 Add the cooked rice to the pan and cook for 2–3 minutes, stirring, or until hot. Add the reserved stock if the mixture gets too sticky.

6 Add the pecorino or Parmesan cheese and mix well.

7 Transfer the risotto to warm serving dishes and serve immediately.

COOK'S TIP

The Genoese are excellent cooks, and they make particularly delicious fish dishes flavoured with the local olive oil.

Risotto-stuffed (Bell) Peppers

Serves 4

INGREDIENTS

4 red or orange (bell) peppers
1 tbsp olive oil
1 large onion, finely chopped
350 g/12 oz arborio (risotto) rice,
    washed
about 15 strands saffron

150 ml/¼ pint white wine
850 ml/1½ pints hot vegetable
    or chicken stock
50 g/1¾ oz/3 tbsp butter
50 g/1¾ oz pecorino cheese,
    grated

50 g/1¾ oz Italian sausage,
    such as felino salame or
    other coarse Italian
    salame, chopped
200 g/7 oz Mozzarella cheese,
    sliced

1 Cut the (bell) peppers in half, retaining some of the stalk. Remove the seeds.

2 Place the (bell) peppers, cut side up, under a preheated grill (broiler) for 12–15 minutes until softened and charred.

3 Meanwhile, heat the oil in a large frying pan (skillet). Add the onion and cook for 3–4 minutes or until softened. Add the rice and saffron, stirring to coat in the oil, and cook for 1 minute.

4 Add the wine and stock slowly, a ladleful at a time, making sure that all of the liquid is absorbed before adding the next ladleful of liquid. When all of the liquid is absorbed, the rice should be cooked. Test by tasting a grain – if it is still crunchy add a little more water and continue cooking. It should take at least 15 minutes to cook.

5 Stir in the butter, pecorino cheese and the chopped Italian sausage.

6 Spoon the risotto into the (bell) peppers. Top

with a slice of Mozzarella and grill (broil) for 4–5 minutes or until the cheese is bubbling. Serve hot.

VARIATION

Use tomatoes instead of the (bell) peppers, if you prefer. Halve 4 large tomatoes and scoop out the seeds. Follow steps 3–6 as there is no need to roast them.

Fresh Baked Sardines

Serves 4

INGREDIENTS

2 tbsp olive oil

2 large onions, sliced into rings

3 garlic cloves, chopped

2 large courgettes (zucchini), cut into sticks

3 tbsp fresh thyme, stalks removed

8 sardine fillets or about 1 kg/2 lb 4 oz whole sardines, filleted

75 g/2³/₄ oz Parmesan cheese, grated

4 eggs, beaten

150 ml/5 fl oz/²/₃ pint milk

salt and pepper

1 Heat 1 tablespoon of the oil in a frying pan (skillet). Add the onions and garlic and sauté for 2–3 minutes.

2 Add the courgettes (zucchini) to the frying pan (skillet) and cook for about 5 minutes or until golden.

3 Stir 2 tablespoons of the thyme into the mixture.

4 Place half of the onions and courgettes (zucchini) in the base of a large ovenproof dish. Top

with the sardine fillets and half of the Parmesan cheese.

5 Place the remaining onions and courgettes (zucchini) on top and sprinkle with the remaining thyme.

6 Mix the eggs and milk together in a bowl and season to taste with salt and pepper. Pour the mixture over the vegetables and sardines in the dish. Sprinkle the remaining Parmesan cheese over the top.

7 Bake in a preheated oven at 180°C/350°F/ Gas Mark 4 for 20–25 minutes or until golden and set. Serve hot, straight from the oven.

VARIATION

If you cannot find sardines that are large enough to fillet, use small mackerel instead.

Rich Beef Stew

Serves 4

INGREDIENTS

1 tbsp oil
15 g/^{1}/$_2$ oz/1 tbsp butter
225 g/8 oz baby onions, peeled
   and halved

600 g/1 lb 5 oz stewing steak, diced
   into 4 cm/1^1/$_2$ inch chunks
300 ml/^{1}/$_2$ pint/1^1/$_4$ cup beef stock
150 ml/5 fl oz/^{2}/$_3$ cup red wine
4 tbsp chopped oregano
1 tbsp sugar

1 orange
25 g/1 oz porcini or other dried
   mushrooms
225 g/8 oz fresh plum tomatoes
cooked rice or potatoes, to serve

1 Heat the oil and butter in a large frying pan (skillet). Add the onions and sauté for 5 minutes or until golden. Remove with a perforated spoon, set aside and keep warm.

2 Add the beef to the pan and cook, stirring, for 5 minutes or until browned all over.

3 Return the onions to the frying pan (skillet) and add the stock, wine, oregano and sugar, stirring to mix well. Transfer the mixture to an ovenproof casserole dish.

4 Pare the rind from the orange and cut it into strips. Slice the orange flesh into rings. Add the orange rings and the rind to the casserole. Cook in a preheated oven, at 180°C/350°F/Gas Mark 4, for 1¼ hours.

5 Soak the porcini mushrooms for 30 minutes in a small bowl containing 4 tablespoons of warm water.

6 Peel and halve the tomatoes. Add the tomatoes, porcini mushrooms and their soaking liquid to the casserole. Cook for a further 20 minutes until the beef is tender and the juices thickened. Serve with cooked rice or potatoes.

VARIATION

Instead of fresh tomatoes, try using 8 sun-dried tomatoes, cut into wide strips, if you prefer.

Pork with Lemon & Garlic

Serves 4

INGREDIENTS

450 g/1 lb pork fillet
50 g/1³/4 oz chopped almonds
2 tbsp olive oil
100 g/3¹/2 oz raw ham
   (prosciutto), finely chopped

2 garlic cloves, chopped
1 tbsp fresh oregano, chopped
finely grated rind of 2 lemons
4 shallots, finely chopped

200 ml/7 fl oz/³/4 cup ham or
   chicken stock
1 tsp sugar

1 Using a sharp knife, cut the pork fillet into 4 equal pieces. Place the pork between sheets of greaseproof paper and pound each piece with a meat mallet or the end of a rolling pin to flatten it.

2 Cut a horizontal slit in each piece of pork to make a pocket.

3 Place the almonds on a baking tray (cookie sheet). Lightly toast the almonds under a medium-hot grill (broiler) for 2–3 minutes or until golden.

4 Mix the almonds with 1 tablespoon of the olive oil, chopped ham (prosciutto), garlic, oregano and the finely grated rind from 1 lemon. Spoon the mixture into the pockets of the pork.

5 Heat the remaining oil in a large frying pan (skillet). Add the shallots and cook for 2 minutes.

6 Add the pork to the frying pan (skillet) and cook for 2 minutes on each side or until browned all over.

7 Add the stock to the pan, bring to the boil, cover and leave to simmer for 45 minutes or until the pork is tender. Remove the meat from the pan, set aside and keep warm.

8 Using a zester, pare the remaining lemon. Add the rind and sugar to the pan, boil for 3–4 minutes or until reduced and syrupy. Pour over the pork fillets and serve immediately.

Neapolitan Pork Steaks

Serves 4

INGREDIENTS

2 tbsp olive oil
1 garlic clove, chopped
1 large onion, sliced
1 x 400 g/14 oz can tomatoes

2 tsp yeast extract
4 pork loin steaks, each about
125 g/4½ oz
75 g/2¾ oz black olives, pitted

2 tbsp fresh basil, shredded
freshly grated Parmesan cheese,
to serve

1 Heat the oil in a large frying pan (skillet). Add the onions and garlic and cook, stirring, for 3–4 minutes or until they just begin to soften.

2 Add the tomatoes and yeast extract to the frying pan (skillet) and leave to simmer for about 5 minutes or until the sauce starts to thicken.

3 Cook the pork steaks, under a preheated grill (broiler), for 5 minutes on both sides, until the the meat is golden and cooked through. Set the pork steaks aside and keep warm.

4 Add the olives and fresh shredded basil to the sauce in the frying pan (skillet) and stir quickly to combine.

5 Transfer the steaks to warm serving plates. Top the steaks with the sauce, sprinkle with freshly grated Parmesan cheese and serve immediately.

COOK'S TIP

Parmesan is a mature and exceptionally hard cheese produced in Italy. You only need to add a little as it has a very strong flavour.

COOK'S TIP

There are many types of canned tomato available – for example plum tomatoes, or tomatoes chopped in water, or chopped sieved tomatoes (passata). The chopped variety are often canned with added flavours such as garlic, basil, onion, chilli and mixed herbs, and are a good storecupboard standby.

Roman Pan-fried Lamb

Serves 4

INGREDIENTS

1 tbsp oil
15 g/¹/₂ oz/1 tbsp butter
600 g/1 lb 5 oz lamb (shoulder or
   leg), cut in 2.5 cm/1 inch chunks
4 garlic cloves, peeled

3 sprigs thyme, stalks removed
6 canned anchovy fillets
150 ml/5 fl oz/²/₃ cup red wine
150 ml/5 fl oz/²/₃ cup lamb or
   vegetable stock

1 tsp sugar
50 g/1³/₄ oz black olives, pitted and
   halved
2 tbsp chopped parsley, to garnish
mashed potato, to serve

1 Heat the oil and butter in a large frying pan (skillet). Add the lamb and cook for 4–5 minutes, stirring, until the meat is browned all over.

2 Using a pestle and mortar, grind together the garlic, thyme and anchovies to make a smooth paste.

3 Add the wine and lamb or vegetable stock to the frying pan (skillet). Stir in the garlic and anchovy paste together with the sugar.

4 Bring the mixture to the boil, reduce the heat, cover and leave to simmer for 30–40 minutes or until the lamb is tender. For the last 10 minutes of the cooking time, remove the lid in order to allow the sauce to reduce slightly.

5 Stir the olives into the sauce and mix to combine.

6 Transfer the lamb and the sauce to a serving bowl and garnish with freshly chopped parsley. Serve with creamy mashed potatoes.

COOK'S TIP

Rome is the capital of both the region of Lazio and Italy and thus has become a focal point for specialities from all over Italy. Food from this region tends to be fairly simple and quick to prepare, all with plenty of herbs and seasonings giving really robust flavours.

Saltimbocca

Serves 4

INGREDIENTS

4 turkey fillets or 4 veal escalopes, about 450 g/1 lb in total
100 g/3³/₄ oz Parma ham (prosciutto)

8 sage leaves
1 tbsp olive oil
1 onion, finely chopped

200 ml/7 fl oz/³/₄ cup white wine
200 ml/7 fl oz/³/₄ cup chicken stock

1 Place the turkey or veal between sheets of greaseproof paper. Pound the meat with a meat mallet or the end of a rolling pin to flatten it slightly. Cut each escalope in half.

2 Trim the Parma ham (prosciutto) to fit each piece of turkey or veal and place over the meat. Lay a sage leaf on top. Roll up the escalopes and secure with a cocktail stick (toothpick).

3 Heat the oil in a frying pan (skillet) and cook the onion for 3–4 minutes. Add the turkey or veal rolls to the pan and cook for 5 minutes until brown all over.

4 Pour the wine and stock into the pan and leave to simmer for 15 minutes if using turkey, and 20 minutes for veal, or until tender. Serve immediately.

VARIATION

Try a similar recipe called Bocconini, *meaning 'little mouthfuls'. Follow the same method as here, but replace the sage leaf with a piece of Gruyère cheese.*

COOK'S TIP

If using turkey rather than veal, watch it carefully as turkey tends to turn dry very quickly if overcooked.

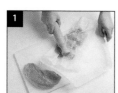

Pizza Margherita

Serves 4

INGREDIENTS

BASIC PIZZA DOUGH:
7 g/1/4 oz dried yeast
1 tsp sugar
250 ml/9 fl oz/1 cup hand-hot water
350 g/12 oz strong flour
1 tsp salt
1 tbsp olive oil

TOPPING:
1 x 400 g/14 oz can tomatoes, chopped
2 garlic cloves, crushed
2 tsp dried basil
1 tbsp olive oil
2 tbsp tomato purée

100 g/3¹/2 oz Mozzarella cheese, chopped
2 tbsp freshly grated Parmesan cheese
salt and pepper

1 Place the yeast and sugar in a measuring jug and mix with 50 ml/2 fl oz/4 tbsp of the water. Leave the yeast mixture in a warm place for 15 minutes or until frothy.

2 Mix the flour with the salt and make a well in the centre. Add the oil, the yeast mixture and the remaining water. Using a wooden spoon, mix to form a dough.

3 Turn the dough out on to a floured surface and knead for 4–5 minutes or until smooth.

4 Return the dough to the bowl, cover with an oiled sheet of cling film (plastic wrap) and leave to rise for 30 minutes or until doubled in size.

5 Knead the dough for 2 minutes. Stretch the dough with your hands, then place it on an oiled baking tray (cookie sheet), pushing out the edges until even and to the shape required. The dough should be no more than 6 mm/¹/4 inch thick because it will rise during cooking.

6 To make the topping, place the tomatoes, garlic, dried basil, olive oil and salt and pepper to taste in a large frying pan (skillet) and leave to simmer for 20 minutes or until the sauce has thickened. Stir in the tomato purée and leave to cool slightly.

7 Spread the topping evenly over the pizza base. Top with the Mozzarella and Parmesan cheeses and bake in a preheated oven at 200°C/400°F/Gas Mark 6 for 20–25 minutes. Serve hot.

Gorgonzola Pizza

Serves 4

INGREDIENTS

PIZZA DOUGH:
7 g/¼ oz dried yeast
1 tsp sugar
250 ml/9 fl oz/1 cup hand-hot water
175 g/6 oz wholemeal flour
175 g/6 oz strong white flour

1 tsp salt
1 tbsp olive oil

TOPPING:
400 g/14 oz pumpkin or squash,
    peeled and cubed

1 tbsp olive oil
1 pear, cored, peeled and sliced
100 g 3½ oz Gorgonzola cheese
1 sprig fresh rosemary, to garnish

1 Place the yeast and sugar in a measuring jug and mix with 50 ml/2 fl oz/4 tbsp of the water. Leave the yeast mixture in a warm place for 15 minutes or until frothy.

2 Mix both of the flours with the salt and make a well in the centre. Add the oil, the yeast mixture and the remaining water. Using a wooden spoon, mix to form a dough.

3 Turn the dough out on to a floured surface and knead for 4–5 minutes or until smooth.

4 Return the dough to the bowl, cover with an oiled sheet of cling film (plastic wrap) and leave to rise for 30 minutes or until doubled in size.

5 Remove the dough from the bowl. Knead the dough for 2 minutes. Using a rolling pin, roll out the dough to form a long oval shape, then place it on an oiled baking tray (cookie sheet), pushing out the edges until even. The dough should be no more than 6 mm/¼ inch thick because it will rise during cooking.

6 To make the topping, place the pumpkin in a shallow roasting tin (pan). Drizzle with the olive oil and cook under a preheated grill (broiler) for 20 minutes or until soft and lightly golden.

7 Top the dough with the pear and the pumpkin, brushing with the oil from the tin (pan). Sprinkle over the Gorgonzola. Bake in a preheated oven, at 200°C/400°F/Gas Mark 6 for 15 minutes or until the base is golden. Garnish with a sprig of rosemary.

Italian Bread Pudding

Serves 4

INGREDIENTS

15 g/¹/₂ oz/1 tbsp butter	2 tbsp white wine	300 ml/¹/₂ pint/1¹/₄ cups single
2 small eating apples, peeled,	100 g/3¹/₂ oz bread, sliced with	(light) cream
cored and sliced into rings	crusts removed (slightly stale	2 eggs, beaten
75 g/2³/₄ oz granulated sugar	French baguette is ideal)	pared rind of 1 orange, cut into
		matchsticks

1 Lightly grease a 1.2 litre/
2 pint deep ovenproof
dish with the butter.

2 Arrange the apple rings
in the base of the dish.
Sprinkle half of the sugar
over the apples.

Pour the wine over
the apple slices.
the slices of bread,
ing them down with
hands to flatten
slightly.

x the cream with
eggs, the remaining
the orange rind
the mixture over

the bread. Leave to soak
for 30 minutes.

5 Bake the pudding in a
preheated oven, at
180°C/350°F/Gas Mark 4,
for 25 minutes until golden
and set. Serve warm.

VARIATION

*For a variation, try adding
dried fruit, such as apricots,
cherries or dates, to the
pudding, if you prefer.*

COOK'S TIP

*Single (light) cream is the
type of cream most commonly
used for cooking. However,
this type of cream should not
be boiled as it will curdle.
Also, always add hot liquids
to the cream rather than the
cream to the liquids, in order
to avoid curdling.
Single (light) cream has an
18 per cent fat content.*

Tuscan Pudding

Serves 4

INGREDIENTS

15 g/½ oz/1 tbsp butter
75 g/2¾ oz mixed dried fruit
250 g/9 oz ricotta cheese

3 egg yolks
50 g/1¾ oz caster (superfine) sugar
1 tsp cinnamon

finely grated rind of 1 orange, plus
extra to decorate
crème fraîche (soured cream),
to serve

1 Lightly grease 4 mini pudding basins or ramekin dishes with the butter.

2 Put the dried fruit in a bowl and cover with warm water. Leave to soak for 10 minutes.

3 Beat the ricotta cheese with the egg yolks in a bowl. Stir in the caster (superfine) sugar, cinnamon and orange rind and mix to combine.

4 Drain the dried fruit in a sieve set over a bowl. Mix the drained fruit with the ricotta cheese mixture.

5 Spoon the mixture into the basins or ramekin dishes.

6 Bake in a preheated oven, at 180°C/350°F/ Gas Mark 4, for 15 minutes. The tops should be firm to the touch but not brown.

7 Decorate the puddings with grated orange rind. Serve warm or chilled with a dollop of crème fraîche (soured cream).

COOK'S TIP

Crème fraîche (soured cream) has a slightly sour, nutty taste and is very thick. It is suitable for cooking, but has the same fat content as double (heavy) cream. It can be made by stirring cultured buttermilk into double (heavy) cream and refrigerating overnight.

VARIATION

Use the dried fruit of your choice for this delicious recipe.

Cream Custards

Serves 4

INGREDIENTS

450 ml/16 fl oz/2 cups single (light) cream	1 orange	1 tbsp honey
100 g/3¾ oz caster (superfine) sugar	2 tsp grated nutmeg	1 tsp cinnamon
	3 large eggs, beaten	

1 Place the cream and sugar in a large non-stick saucepan and heat gently, stirring, until the sugar caramelizes.

2 Finely grate half of the orange rind and add it to the pan along with the nutmeg.

3 Add the eggs to the mixture in the pan and cook over a low heat for 10–15 minutes, stirring constantly. The custard will eventually thicken.

4 Strain the custard through a fine sieve, into 4 shallow serving dishes. Leave to chill in the refrigerator for 2 hours.

5 Meanwhile, pare the remaining orange rind and cut it into matchsticks.

6 Place the honey and cinnamon in a pan with 2 tablespoons of water and heat gently. Add the orange rind to the pan and cook for 2–3 minutes, stirring, until the mixture has caramelized.

7 Pour the mixture into a bowl and separate out the orange sticks. Leave to cool until set.

8 Once the custards have set, decorate them with the caramelized orange rind and serve.

COOK'S TIP

The cream custards will keep for 1–2 days in the refrigerator. Decorate with the caramelized orange rind just before serving.

Sicilian Orange & Almond Cake

Serves 8

INGREDIENTS

4 eggs, separated
125 g/4$^1/_2$ oz caster (superfine)
    sugar, plus 2 tsp for the cream
finely grated rind and juice of
    2 oranges

finely grated rind and juice of
    1 lemon
125 g/4$^1/_2$ oz ground almonds
25 g/1 oz self-raising flour
200 ml/7 fl oz/$^3/_4$ cup whipping
    (light) cream

1 tsp cinnamon
25 g/1 oz flaked (slivered)
    almonds, toasted
icing (confectioners') sugar, to dust

1 Grease and line the base of a 18 cm/7 inch round deep cake tin (pan).

2 Blend the egg yolks with the sugar until the mixture is thick and creamy. Whisk half of the orange rind and all of the lemon rind into the egg yolks.

3 Mix the juice from both oranges and the lemon with the ground almonds and stir into the egg yolks. The mixture will become quite runny at this point. Fold in the flour.

4 Whisk the egg whites until stiff and gently fold into the egg yolk mixture.

5 Pour the mixture into the tin (pan) and bake in a preheated oven, at 180°C/350°F/Gas Mark 4, for 35–40 minutes, until golden and springy to the touch. Leave to cool in the tin (pan) for 10 minutes and then turn out. It is likely to sink slightly at this stage.

6 Whip the cream to form soft peaks. Stir in the remaining orange rind, cinnamon and sugar.

7 Once the cake is cold, cover with the toasted almonds, dust with icing (confectioners') sugar and serve with the cream.

VARIATION

You could serve this cake with a syrup. Boil the juice and finely grated rind of 2 oranges, 75 g/2¾ oz caster (superfine) sugar and 2 tbsp of water for 5–6 minutes until slightly thickened. Stir in 1 tbsp of orange liqueur just before serving.

Zabaglione

Serves 4

INGREDIENTS

5 egg yolks	150 ml/ 5 fl oz/²/₃ cup Marsala or	amaretti biscuits, to serve
100 g/3¹/₂ oz caster (superfine) sugar	sweet sherry	(optional)

1 Place the egg yolks in a large mixing bowl.

2 Add the caster (superfine) sugar to the egg yolks and whisk until the mixture is thick and very pale and has doubled in volume.

3 Place the bowl containing the egg yolk and sugar mixture over a saucepan of gently simmering water.

4 Add the Marsala or sherry to the egg yolk and sugar mixture and continue whisking until the foam mixture becomes warm. This process may take as long as 10 minutes.

5 Pour the mixture, which should be frothy and light, into 4 wine glasses.

6 Serve the zabaglione warm with fresh fruit or amaretti biscuits, if you wish.

VARIATION

Any other type of liqueur may be used instead of the Marsala or sweet sherry, if you prefer. Serve soft fruits, such as strawberries or raspberries, with the zabaglione – it's a delicious combination!

VARIATION

Iced or Semifreddo Zabaglione can be made by following the method here, then continuing to whisk the foam while standing the bowl in cold water. Beat 150 ml/¹/₄ pint/²/₃ cup whipping (light) cream until it just holds its shape. Fold into the foam and freeze for about 2 hours, until just frozen.

Lemon Mascarpone Cheesecake

Serves 8

INGREDIENTS

50 g/1¾ oz/1½ tbsp unsalted butter
150 g/5½ oz ginger biscuits
  (cookies), crushed

25 g/1 oz stem ginger (candied),
  chopped
500 g/1 lb 2 oz mascarpone cheese

finely grated rind and juice of 2 lemons
100 g/3½ oz caster (superfine) sugar
2 large eggs, separated
fruit coulis (see Cook's Tip), to serve

1 Grease and line the base of a 25 cm/10 inch spring-form cake tin (pan) or loose-bottomed tin (pan).

2 Melt the butter in a pan and stir in the crushed biscuits (cookies) and chopped ginger. Use the mixture to line the tin (pan), pressing the mixture about 6 mm/¼ inch up the sides.

3 Beat together the cheese, lemon rind and juice, sugar and egg yolks until smooth.

4 Whisk the egg whites until they are stiff and fold into the cheese and lemon mixture.

5 Pour the mixture into the tin (pan) and bake in a preheated oven, at180°C/350°F/Gas Mark 4, for 35–45 minutes until just set. Don't worry if it cracks or sinks – this is quite normal.

6 Leave the cheesecake in the tin (pan) to cool. Serve with fruit coulis (see Cook's Tip).

COOK'S TIP

Fruit coulis can be made by cooking 400 g/14 oz fruit, such as blueberries, for 5 minutes with 2 tablespoons of water. Sieve the mixture, then stir in 1 tablespoon (or more to taste) of sifted icing (confectioners') sugar. Leave to cool before serving.

VARIATION

Ricotta cheese can be used instead of the mascarpone to make an equally delicious cheesecake. However, it should be sieved before use to remove any lumps.

Granita

Serves 4

INGREDIENTS

LEMON GRANITA:	COFFEE GRANITA:
3 lemons	2 tbsp instant coffee
200 ml/7 fl oz/³/₄ cup lemon juice	2 tbsp sugar
100 g/3¹/₂ oz caster (superfine) sugar	2 tbsp hot water
500 ml/18 fl oz/2¹/₄ cups cold water	600 ml/1 pint/2¹/₂ cups cold water
	2 tbsp rum or brandy

1 To make lemon granita, finely grate the lemon rind. Place the lemon rind, juice and caster (superfine) sugar in a pan. Bring the mixture to the boil and leave to simmer for 5-6 minutes or until thick and syrupy. Leave to cool.

2 Once cooled, stir in the cold water and pour into a shallow freezer container with a lid. Freeze the granita for 4-5 hours, stirring occasionally to break up the ice. Serve as a palate cleanser between dinner courses.

3 To make coffee granita, place the coffee and sugar in a bowl and pour over the hot water, stirring until dissolved.

4 Stir in the cold water and rum or brandy.

5 Pour the mixture into a shallow freezer container with a lid. Freeze the granita for at least 6 hours, stirring every 1–2 hours in order to create a grainy texture. Serve with cream after dinner, if you wish.

COOK'S TIP

If you would prefer a non-alcoholic version of the coffee granita, simply omit the rum or brandy and add extra instant coffee instead.

This is a Parragon Book
First published in 2000

Parragon
Queen Street House
4 Queen Street
Bath BA1 1HE, UK

ISBN: 0-75253-619-2

Printed in China

Note

Cup measurements in this book are for American cups. Tablespoons are assumed to be
15 ml. Unless otherwise stated, milk is assumed to be full fat, eggs are medium and
pepper is freshly ground black pepper.